Giant Crabs and Spiders

Robin Thomas spent most of his working life in an engineering company in Reading having qualified as a chemical engineer at Birmingham University. While still employed, he obtained a degree in English Studies from the then Polytechnic of North London, followed by an MA in Victorian Poetry at the Open University and an MA in Writing Poetry at Kingston University. He lives in Caversham, Reading.

For Horace
looking forward to
seeing you at Christmas time
Robin
Nov '25

Giant Crabs and Spiders

Robin Thomas

TWO RIVERS PRESS

By the same author

Poetry

A Fury of Yellow (Eyewear, 2016)
Momentary Turmoil (Cinnamon, 2018)
A Distant Hum (Cinnamon, 2021)
Cafferty's Truck (Dempsey and Windle, 2021)
The Weather on the Moon (Two Rivers Press, 2022)
Reminded of Something (Cinnamon, 2023)

Flash Fiction Novellas

Margot and the Strange Objects (Adhoc, 2022)
The Lion, the Lord, the Lower Orders and the Belt and Road Initiative (Alien Buddha, 2024)

Also by Two Rivers Poets

David Attwooll, *The Sound Ladder* (2015)
Charles Baudelaire, *Paris Scenes* translated by Ian Brinton (2021)
William Bedford, *The Dancers of Colbek* (2020)
Kate Behrens, *Man with Bombe Alaska* (2016)
Kate Behrens, *Penumbra* (2019)
Kate Behrens, *Transitional Spaces* (2022)
Conor Carville, *English Martyrs* (2019)
David Cooke, *A Murmuration* (2015)
David Cooke, *Sicilian Elephants* (2021)
Tim Dooley, *Discoveries* (2022)
Jane Draycott, *Tideway* (re-issued 2022)
Jane Draycott & Lesley Saunders, *Christina the Astonishing* (re-issued 2022)
Claire Dyer, *Yield* (2021)
Claire Dyer, *The Adjustments* (2024)
John Froy, *Sandpaper & Seahorses* (2018)
John Froy, *The Blue Armchair* (2024)
James Harpur, *The Examined Life* (2021)
James Harpur, *The Magic Theatre* (2025)
Kitty Hawkins, *These Yellow Days* (2025)
Maria Teresa Horta, *Point of Honour* translated by Lesley Saunders (2019)

Ian House, *Just a Moment* (2020)
Philippe Jaccottet, *In Winter Light* translated by Tim Dooley (2022)
Rosie Jackson, *Love Leans over the Table* (2023)
Rosie Jackson & Graham Burchell, *Two Girls and a Beehive: Poems about Stanley Spencer and Hilda Carline* (2020)
Martha Kapos, *Music, Awake Her* (2024)
Gill Learner, *Chill Factor* (2016)
Gill Learner, *Change* (2021)
Sue Leigh, *Chosen Hill* (2018)
Sue Leigh, *Her Orchards* (2021)
Becci Louise, *Octopus Medicine* (2017)
Mairi MacInnes, *Amazing Memories of Childhood, etc.* (2016)
Steven Matthews, *On Magnetism* (2017)
Steven Matthews, *Some Other Where* (2023)
Katherine Meehan, *Dame Julie Andrews' Botched Vocal Cord Surgery and Other Poems* (2023)
Henri Michaux, *Storms under the Skin* translated by Jane Draycott (2017)
Kate Noakes, *Goldhawk Road* (2023)
Alistair Noon, *Paradise Takeaway* (2023)
René Noyau, *Earth on Fire and other Poems* translated by Gérard Noyau with Peter Pegnall (2021)
Ruth O'Callaghan, *Where Shadow Falls* (2023)
James Peake, *Reaction Time of Glass* (2019)
James Peake, *The Star in the Branches* (2022)
James Peake, *The Third City* (2025)
David Ricks, *With Signs Following* (2024)
Peter Robinson & David Inshaw, *Bonjour Mr Inshaw* (2020)
Peter Robinson, *English Nettles* (re-issued 2022)
Peter Robinson, *Retrieved Attachments* (2023)
Lesley Saunders, *Nominy-Dominy* (2018)
Lesley Saunders, *This Thing of Blood & Love* (2022)
Jack Thacker, *Handling* (2018)
Susan Utting, *The Colour of Rain* (2024)
Jean Watkins, *Precarious Lives* (2018)

First published in the UK in 2025 by Two Rivers Press
7 Denmark Road, Reading RG1 5PA
www.tworiverspress.com
info@tworiverspress.com

General Product Safety Regulations (GPSR) documentation:
www.tworiverspress.com/about/gpsr

EU GPSR Authorised Representative:
Logos Europe Ltd
9 Rue Nicolas Poussin, 17000 La Rochelle, France
contact@logoseurope.eu

ISBN 978-1-915048-29-5

1 2 3 4 5 6 7 8 9

Two Rivers Press is represented in the UK by Inpress Ltd and distributed by BookSource, Glasgow.

Cover illustration and design by Sally Castle
Text design by Nadja Robinson and typeset in Janson and Parisine

Printed and bound in Great Britain by CMP (UK), Poole

Acknowledgements

Thanks to my many friends on the poetry scenes in Reading, Bath, London and elsewhere. Thanks are also due to the editors of the following in which some of these poems previously appeared: *Acumen, Agenda, Envoi, Orbis, Brittle Star, Pennine Platform, The High Window, Poetry Scotland, South, Poetry Salzburg Review, Stand, Rialto, The Interpreter's House, North, Tears in the Fence* and *The Frogmore Papers*.

For Mary,
who died in October 2021

Contents

I. Opposable Thumbs

II. Quince, Apples and Pears

III. Poached Egg

IV. Almost Everyone Excluded

I. Opposable Thumbs

Transcendental Preserve

'I get it, Manny, we can't
know further than our noses, not to mention
eyes and ears etc,' and the four boys
walked on, pondering, over fields, hills and valleys,
filling their lungs with air, listening to the birds,
feeling the energy in their limbs as they went.
'But Manny,' said John, 'I've been giving it
a lot of thought, in fact I've already got
several thick notebooks about it on the go
and I reckon that that
undifferentiated, immaterial, timeless, spaceless something
you go on about can only be full of
marmalade.' On they went
as the sun went down, seeing the flowers
folding, watching the rabbits hopping to and fro.
At length Freddie spoke:
'What kind of marmalade?' he asked.
'Well,' said George, after a long pause,
'Could it be ginger?' 'That's never marmalade!
Must be made of oranges – bitter or Seville!'
'Naah,' said John, 'too traditional.' 'Could be
Valencia or navel,' Freddie said. 'Too sweet,'
was George's view. 'Grapefruit or kumquat
might work, or lemon or lime,' wondered John.
'Nope. Has to be ginger, you won't ever
have one of them Copernican revolutions
with Seville.'

A New Leaf

I. The end of history

No wonder leaves are angry: no longer
content to live and fall, live and fall,
they've been studying Hegel – there isn't
much else for them to do, not having
opposable thumbs. Yes, leaves
are easily bored. Now they're
angry *and* bored, for Hegel
has instilled in them knowledge
of their Being, including – blimey! –
that they're mortal. 'Nobody
ever told us that! How dare they
create us under false pretences, we mean,
without telling us what they've let us in for?

'We used to wonder why those strange
creatures with moving trunks
get so cross all the time. Now we know.'

II. If you stand very still

'Now hang on a minute,' said
an old, brown, mottled bent leaf,
'you may be mortal but you are immortal too,
if you behave yourselves.' 'Eh, how's that,'
unisoned the others.' 'Just look around you:
at the other trees, the grass, those
hopping rabbits blah blah. You don't need
Hegel, you need Patience Strong.' 'Tell us
about her.' they chorused.
There was a kind of eager silence.
Crepitation turned to rustling. 'We like that.'
they all said and as the old leaf
conducted them they turned
this way and that, that way and this
and promised not to misbehave.

The Doors of Perception

Doors closing. *Thank you lift.*
You're welcome. *Thank you again.*
Not everyone thanks me.
The world is an awful place.
Isn't it. But some things are good.
Lifts are good. Yes lifts are good,
although not absolutely always.
No? No, sometimes we
trap your fingers, or refuse
to move, or go somewhere
you don't want us to. We
can even break down, though
that's not usually our fault;
it's usually the fault of the world
being an awful place.

The Assassination of St Peter Martyr

Giovanni Bellini, *c.* 1505

'Universal compassion is the only guarantee of morality'
— Arthur Schopenhauer, *On the Basis of Morality* (1839)

That all is one, he says,
is the fountain of our care
for one another, for all things,
of all things for all things, why,
those trees, bustled together,
have spread out their leaves
to screen from an absent creator
those who murder, hack and beat
themself.

First Open the Box

You might need a sharp knife
but if you do,
be careful not to damage what's inside,
or indeed cut your finger(s).
Take the contents out and lay each piece
on a horizontal surface, such as a floor
(yes, of course, it has to be big enough!)
Compare each piece with the list
included in the envelope,
there it is, look, crumpled at the end.
If any pieces are missing contact us immediately!
We will respond as soon as we can, although
we are currently experiencing a high volume of calls.

Lay down long piece *a*
Find piece *b* (it will have a notch in it)
and insert it into the matching slot in *a*.
Twist *c* so that it slides between *a* and *b*.
You'll have to tap it gently with
special tool *t1* (not provided).
On no account push it too far, it will get stuck
and you will *never* be able to get it out.
Continue in a similar manner with *d* and *e*,
Then *f* to *q*, *s* to *w1*, *w2 to 14*, *y1* to 47 and finally, *z*
and all its sub-parts and assemblies,
assigns and successors. (It's not yet assembled
– see instruction manual section FAQ).
Careful. I said careful!

As long as you *are* careful
And follow these instructions to the letter
(Watch out! Do not allow your finger
To get stuck between pieces *w13* and *y34*.
It's easily done – one of these days we'll fix it),
it will all come together quite nicely
and might give you faithful service for many years
although we don't recommend
that you prolong your life to an inordinate extent,
just in case.

A Window

is a device for keeping things out
and also in
while pretending it's not there.
You can open a window
so that it really isn't there, alternatively
you can pull curtains over a window
to pretend it's not pretending
not to be there.

The birches in next door's garden
can be seen equally well
whether the window is or isn't there,
insofar as they are really there
which is a metaphysical issue
beyond the scope of a discussion
of windows, which should more properly
have to do with their type, the materials
used in their manufacture
and their history, which would be
bound to refer to the window tax that
everyone's heard of, pointing out,
as they drive by in their Vauxhalls,
windows bricked up for that purpose
and only referred to now as windows
in a problematic sense.

Souls have windows into them.
This is an instance of something
pretending not to be there
at the very moment it permits visual access
to something that really isn't there.

Tale of the Dog

after Christopher Reid, 'A Wagtail Sonnet'

'words are more sweet, and here I proffer proofs,
One witty word is worth a thousand woofs.'

'One witty word
is worth a thousand woofs' says Reid.
What does he know? Each Woof
may carry a world of information, or
nothing. We cannot tell, unless a Martian,
skilled in languages, create a new Rosetta Stone,
with Woof, a Martian tongue, and English,
say, or Tibetan, or Navajo, and send it
spinning through our common space
to crash into the ocean, where fishermen,
cowering at first from the explosion in the sea,
haul it in for profit, or in wonder.

A new Champollion, arriving at the beach,
on holiday perhaps, in bright coloured shirt
and cargo shorts, takes charge. These days
all he has to do is load the symbols
for each language into his phone and hey presto,
we can speak, well, one dialect of Martian,
and, er, one of Woof which may be
philosophical, or sound and fury only.

The Glass of Water

It's protected from gravity
by the sides and bottom
of the glass, but if you think of it
as two adjacent vertical bodies then each
is also protecting the other. If
it were thought of as
a large number of such bodies,
then there would be a lot
of protecting going on.

I am protected from thoughts
of mortality by a kind of glass wall
which surrounds me on all sides.
If there were
a very large number of us,
as indeed there are,
we could all protect each other
and go down the hill
to the church together,
on a Sunday perhaps,
the walls of the church
standing in for the glass.

If the glass bottom
were very extensive indeed
and if that huge number of water-entities
were to rely entirely on each other
for their protection from gravity,
it is possible to imagine a continuous body of water,
of a depth of just a few centimetres
extending right round the world.
Much good it would do them –
the world is not used to
the kind of steadiness
that would be required.

Getting There

They've put bollards in the road
which has silenced it.
You could walk I suppose
but no one would.

You can still go in other directions
by car or bus and you can
get there by train, until
they blow up the bridge.

Better stay at home then,
getting those household tasks done,
the distances, between
kitchen and bedroom for instance,

being more than manageable – it's
a long way there on foot,
and who would want to go
anywhere else?

What Can Be Said

'Whereof we cannot speak, thereof we must remain silent'
— Wittgenstein, *Tractatus Logico-Philosophicus*

'Girls can't do Euclid, can they sir?'
'They can pick up a little of everything, I daresay,' said Mr Stelling. 'They've a great deal of superficial cleverness: but they couldn't go far into anything. They're quick and shallow.'
— George Eliot, *The Mill on the Floss* (1860)

Mr Stelling worked for years
towards these words, assembling
as he went a mountain
of data in support, making conjecture
upon conjecture, subjecting them
he thought, to all possible refutations.
And so he toiled and toiled, until at last
he satisfied himself
that all challenges had failed: Stelling
had earned the right
to release into the world
his wise words.

Spurred on by this success, Stelling
was indefatigable. More years,
more work, more
mind-stretching effort,
more piles of evidence,
gave him, he felt, the right to say
with absolute confidence:

'Rappognerp smangleplig xog lop!
Bape mrapstlell apropable knee.'

Ball Games

The ship strikes the sea which
rattles its bones, holds, lets
go as it slides
into the white-streaked trough.
The physicists struggle to keep
their balance as they
smash their balls against the shifting walls,
the ceiling, and even sometimes
the table.

A glance and Michael is ready to go,
sets up his shot –
no top, bottom, draw back,
sidespin shots for him –
the ball travels
to its pre-ordained place
on the perfect summer's day of
the table.

II. Quince, Apples and Pears

How to Read a Poem

First see if there are any crocodiles in it, or any other Dendrobatidae Dendrobates or similar. Watch out: these animals are dangerous! Or there might be those red flowers that nobody knows the name of. Look out too for clouds of words – remember, every cloud has a lining of some kind. While we're on the subject of words, count them! If there are 87 or a subdivided multiple thereof it is a short poem. Do not be afraid. Count them again and sort them into sheep. Finally, you may find some meaning mixed in with the Christmas jumpers, bottle tops and hub caps. But probably not.

The Black Birds

I.

As I looked about me
all I saw
was winter shadow.

II.

I shovelled stuff
into sacks of time but
not everything would fit.

III.

Were we one?

Now
I am one.

IV.

The black birds
spin and circle,
searching, searching,

V.

their
labyrinthine complexity
exclusively focussed.

VI.

We are simple creatures.
Why then
this burden,

VII.

the savage burden of thought
under whose weight we must
labour?

VIII.

I hate them,
the birds,
soaring and circling.

IX.

I am
reminded, the birds
are not.

X.

There is not much alternative
to life. I know it.
The birds live it.

XI.

It is April. I must
lift myself up. I must
wade through cruelty.

XII.

It changes every day,
but not
for the birds?

XIII.

Kindness waits
by the unlocked door.
The birds are free in their cages.

The Devil's Bridge

J. M. W. Turner (1802)

'[the Alps are] a pleasure to the eye, ... but mingled with horrours'
— John Dennis, *Miscellanies in Prose and Verse* (1693)

Nothing but mountain, heav-
ing out of the picture, except
gorge, lost beneath it, and
a few persons,
tiny as bristle strokes,
who approach
on a cramped path,
high above
the river that may be down there,
a strand of bridge
pulled tight across the void,
quivering
in the swirling sublimity,
making ready ...

Damaged

Edward Bawden, 'European Ward, South African 18th, Casualty Clearing Station, Maaten Bagush' (*c.* 1942)

A note on the back of the drawing states: 'damaged by sea water'

He saved it
from the torpedo that sank him,
and from Vichy which
fished him out
as the wounded he had drawn
were saved to fight again
in the heat, flies and bullets
of North Africa: an image of men
who would die for freedom,
or go home, back to farms
or offices or the SAP.

SAP South African Police

Schubert's Piano Sonata in B-flat Major, Opus D960

His last sonata
is not his last, although
it is his last.

Mountains, forests, the shimmering lake
if you like, or
molto moderato if you prefer,

but not a testament
or farewell,
although it is his last.

Sweet Suede

Another purchase, of some suede shoes – then a rarity, proved less fortunate: one shoe split the next day, and Nora went back to the store with Kathleen to exchange them. When the manager was reluctant, Nora said, 'My husband is a writer and if you don't change them I'll have it published in the paper.' This was perhaps the only occasion on which Nora spoke of her husband's occupation with approval ...'
— Richard Elman, *James Joyce* (1959)

How sweet her husband once,
the before writer, writer now of
oh so difficult, so thick, enormous books.
Suede shoe split is suede shoe split.
Who reads those great gravins o' books
piled on my table? I'd rather have suede
on my feet or swede or suet or sweets
on my table than swathes of books.
Should have married a non-book man,
a newspaper, racing page, football
man than ..., useful as it was
to have him today.

Barracão

Elizeth's voice
holds up each new roof
while Jorge's mandolin
floats in and out,
bringing,
to hold them down,
nails,
which are driven
one   three four,
one   three four;
nails found
in alleyways
in rubbish dumps
and in the hands
of Nosso Senhor.

barracão (Brazilian Portuguese): 'zinc slum'. 'Zinc' refers to the corrugated galvanised steel roofs ubiquitous on slum dwellings in the favelas of Rio de Janeiro

To Daskalos

after Andrew Marvell, 'To His Coy Mistress' (1681)

Were we not reasonable and fair,
our souls untrammelled as the air,
had we not learnt at parents' knee
good and godly souls to be,
our needs and wants to repudiate
our only charge our neighbour's fate,
for universal justice hunt
and peace to bring to every front
we *might* employ those wondrous jewels
our finest English public schools.

But as we are such, let us seek
to pay for the friendless and the weak
to go to Eton, there to praise
fagging, dormitories, Grecian ways,
teachers whose liking is the cane
their pleasure maximising pain,
the teaching – it is immanent –
that those outside aren't worth a cent,
these to imbibe and come to see
that they can be as good as we.

Cézanne and the Foundations of Mathematics

Two apples on a table – two
Still life with quince, apples and pears – three
Still life with apples – six
Still life with seven apples – seven
The basket of apples – twenty-two

He counts with his brush,
avant Russell and the *Principles*,
that vast book that would prove,
well, fail to prove,
that two plus two equals four.

Painting and counting,
painting, counting, then
passing the baton to the great man in Cambridge,
like him falling short, like him
triumphing.

More Quartets

T.S. Eliot, 'East Coker' (1940)

Dear Mr Eliot, please do not forget
the factory workers, car mechanics,
day labourers, dustmen, shop assistants,
miners, long distance lorry drivers,
housewives with part time jobs
and these days piece workers in the gig economy,
and all the other less than grand
who troop, exhausted,
having no time for mental emptiness
or to think about nothing, and
not much time for love and hope,
into the dark, there, one might hope,
to find respite from the demands
of the captains and merchant bankers,
industrial lords, statesmen, rulers
and their ilk who so proudly precede them,
or perhaps you might think that 'the
whisper of running streams' is not for them.

Long Island Heaven

Joaquin Sorolla y Bastida, *Louis Comfort Tiffany* (1911)

Never mind angels and archangels,
spirits, saints, souls and so on,
here are flowers of wondrous size,
hue and profusion, a sea of celestial blue,
an island out of Homer, a suit of purest white,
a doting, stylish dog, and brush, palette,
easel (turned away in case perfection's
not yet arrived at): the pastime of angels.

How he smiles. Wouldn't you?
Looks like he owns it.
Perhaps he does.

Appeal

The Bowl of Milk, *Pierre Bonnard* (1919)

She enters my dream,
flooding it with the colours of night:
browns and blues, eerie light and shadows.
Asleep, she holds a bowl, nothing to do
with the breakfast things,
which in any case are about to slide off the table,
crash out of the picture. No, she offers it
to me. It is a sort of misty, shadowy
somnambulistic plea. Perhaps
she thinks I can help her cast off her mistiness,
become flesh and blood; or perhaps
resolve herself
into sharp intersecting planes of colour,
leave behind the burden she feels so heavily,
of representing something.

The Barrage Balloon

Leslie Cole, *Working Inside a Balloon* (1941)

Such is their concentration that the WAAFs are unaware of the shadows cast on the balloon's skin. In due course they will look up and smile: 'Look at the shadows, Mavis,' one might say, 'they really look like giant crabs and spiders, don't they.' 'They certainly do, Dorothy,' the other might return. What they will find when they finish their work and go outside is not known.

Performances

Marina Abramović, *Royal Academy* (2023)

They walk the great wall of China,
ninety miles each, converging
on marriage. Ninety miles –
of brick, stone, battlements,
towers, levels, slopes, steps up
and down, aching emptiness,
people who stare – is a long way.
Too long in fact.

Now she rests, lying for ever
on a platform raised above
a stony beach,
by a shushing sea,
the only movement
her hair responding to a breeze.
From a bench they share
with crystals of quartz, visitors
watch, contemplate their auras,
consult their phones.

Captain

after W. H. Henley, 'Invictus' (1888)

'I am the master of my fate,
I am the captain of my soul.'

Sometimes it's night, quite black
  unless the moon is out, or it's daytime
and I beg the gods to leave my soul,
  whatever that may be, alone.

Things change, at times
  I'm held fast in circumstance, or nature,
at others I stride free, either way, I'm
  sometimes bowed, sometimes not,

often a bit of both. I do my best
  considering my destination
which I don't like the sound of much
  and fear when I remember it.

I suppose it's really all a bit of fun for them
  who let me feel I'm in charge
just at the point when they, giggling,
  pissing, puking, take hold of the rug.

The great poet contemplates mortality: its inevitability, his acceptance of it, the last things, what may come after, his effects, his legacy

Actually I think I'd like to
die in bed. Preferably
someone else's.

III. Poached Egg

Supermarket

He went shopping, went to purchase sustaining provender,
drove to the car park, steered that extension of his body
into a space, parking precisely between the white lines.
He took the empty shopping bags, bags devoid of content
and entered the supermarket, among the cornucopia
of foodstuffs, of the wherewithal to maintain life,
went from aisle to aisle, selecting what he needed
and took them to the till, to exchange money for them.
Then he went to his house, went home,
returned to his empty house, that used to be home.

Impact

It's all new here,
though quite familiar,
all the elements being as before;
I say all,
but mean most – there's

a new absence casting itself about,
knocking everything down with its
heavy roundness, each thing
bobbing up again, nodding, swaying,
familiar, unfamiliar.

Reflections

As I walk along the river,

children who chatter
bubbles of strollers
cyclists impervious
runners imperious
the sun slightly too bright
breeze
wavelets
geese staring sullen
a bobbing swan
a boat
another boat

I remember.

Poached Egg

To push his mother up the ramp
through the unwilling doors
and watch her
try to eat a poached egg
was hard.

Visiting Hour

I had TB when I was two and shouldn't really be here
but I am, I'm pleased on balance to say, thanks
to the doctors. My mum, who may have miscarried around then –
I don't know, she never said, but she mentioned something
to Mary about it before they both died – was allowed
to peek through a little window, although she was advised
not to attract my attention 'in case it upset me' (in those days
people did everything the doctor said). Now it's late – I'm
in my seventies and it's four o'clock and my mum has left.

An Essex Childhood

When I think of my childhood in Essex –
where our journey out of the East End
had taken us, of Hillside Avenue that I used to
run across to play with David
and cycle along to school; that dad
drove home to from London, tired as hell,
to leave after dinner to help build
the swimming pool at the school
while I was doing the homework
which would prepare me for a further journey,
as if our life in Hillside Avenue
had no meaning except as a staging post –
I remember yes, the Saturday morning cricket,
the cider, the trips to London for the jazz clubs,
the failed attempts to mate, but mostly a haze
giving way to aspirations become concrete, like
sturdy columns waiting for something to support.

hampton

'... we must consider what Person stands for ... the same thinking thing in different times and places....'
— John Locke, 'An Essay concerning Human Understanding' (1694)

First ball – spinning stumps,
and hampton begins
the long walk back. He
is clapped all the way, his
face a picture as he
climbs the steps
amid enthusiastic applause
and back-slaps.

What fun, what joy,
to list ourselves, though just
grammar school boys
paid for by Beveridge:
M.J. Butterworth Esq.,
P.W.E. Dankworth Esq.,
David Hughes Esq.,
and he, the eleventh,
hampton.

hampton is with me now,
hampton is always with me,
though I don't know
where he went, and didn't
think I cared.
                                        But I'd like
to meet him once more,
to award him, amid applause,
his 'H', to give him not out.

Hostilities

Hector was already at least thirty
when auntie Helen passed him
on to us, God knows how old he is now.
Later on we got another from *Penny's Pets*
to keep him company, Achilles, his name was.
They're still there in the garden,
usually rootling amongst the foliage
and you have to make sure you don't step on them
when you walk along the path. This afternoon

we went up to the lake and took
never-to-be-looked-at photos of what you thought
were rare orchids, taking care not to tread
on the buttercups spread out around them
in temporary glory. On our return
we had a big argument about something
and you ended up heaving a soup ladle
in my direction. It missed and landed
harmlessly near the unconcerned creatures.

Thanks to Spruce Pets: 'A–Z of names for turtles and tortoises'

Why is the Universe so Annoying?

I mean the dishwasher door
bashes me on the shin every time
I walk past. I could close it I suppose
but that's just more time wasted:
why should I have to open it, close it,
open it every time I've got a dirty mug?
Talking about waste, why can't all those
planets and things just stop spinning
all over the place for a moment?
It makes me dizzy, and uses up
all that energy to boot, Some of it
could be used to lighten our evenings
in December, which is otherwise
a very aggravating month. And another thing:
when I'm on a train why do all those people
have to go up and down, up and down the aisle,
brushing against me and sometimes
knocking my elbow? Couldn't there be a force
which glues people to their seats
while they're travelling? And as for Susan,
why doesn't she call me back?

The End of my Holiday

I'm nearing the end of my holiday.
I've had such fun: paddling,
swimming, walking along the front
the sun high in the blue sky;
building castles with the children,
buying them ice-cream, jaunts
into the countryside, fish and chips
on the harbour wall.

Soon it will be time to go,
It's into the car, leaving
Jenny, the children, all my stuff,
everyone, outside, waving as I go.

Metronome

'If you can't play it,'
said Schnabel,
'slow down
until you can.' So I
slow down the metronome,
click, click .. click … click
and try again, and
again. Then, when I'm
ready for my cup of tea
I stop it with my finger,
leaving it quivering,
and soon, still.

But if I've set it really low,
after the quiver stops,
it sometimes starts again,
ready to continue
until the spring runs down:
click … click,
click … … … click,
click … … … … … click,
click.

Room with a View

My birches are blossoming
in orange yellow. I have never
seen such beauty. But, mutton,
they are clothed as lamb: *Look at me,*
at me, choosy Sun, they say, as they
prepare to dismember themselves,
millions of death making way for new life.

Stay out there! Don't
come in here with your metaphors.
Let them pile up
at your indifferent feet. Yesterday,
they were your children,
silently chattering. Now
look what you've done! Look
what you've done to me, God!

Boing

Those who live here
go there every day
by car or train
here there here there as if
in the grip of a rubber band –
boing boing boing boing

or take their young
every day
by car, or walking
from here to other theres
here there here there –
twang twang twang twang.

Later they go
to yet different theres
by car usually or bus –
here there here there
until they're there more than here – as if
in the clutch of an elastic band
until it snaps.

IV. Almost Everyone Excluded

The Not Quite-ness of Things

like the 'not *quite* yet' of Celia Johnson
in Brief Encounter as she contemplates
an ordinary life; like Oswald's feather
'not quite in full possession' of its weight;
or like my porridge – not quite ready
although I've got to go; or like
the thousand things to do
before I die, which are, well,
not quite started; or like
our masters who may not quite
be honest or not quite competent,
or human and who, when the tempests
and the floods and the droughts come,
will not quite be able to save us.

That Was the Day the Trees Started Talking,

birches to birches first, oaks to oaks,
then Scotch pines to Irish, chestnut
to plane, then plane to roses, shrubs, grass,
grass to rabbit, rabbit to bird, bird
to cat, cat to dog, dog
to human, well they do that anyway;
the point is that all the living elements
of the world, big, small and medium,
became engaged in a
great, flowing, mellifluous conversation,
about? well, topics too numerous to name.
'Oh, before, I thought you were just a tree,'
might say a snail, 'and I just thought
you were a house moving company,'
might reply a birch and they would chuckle
and begin to exchange ideas: 'if you lifted up
those roots, you could move like me,' …
'if you put that house down you could come up
and see the world like I can.' And 'I just thought
you were taking the piss with your hopping about,'
said the bird to the rabbit, 'and I thought you
were only flying to avoid me. Come down
and perch here.' 'I will if you'll stop jumping around.'
Even human began to talk to human:
'Before, I thought you were just a Tory,
selfishly wanting everything for yourself,' …
'and I thought you were just a lazy so and so
and wanted what my dad had earnt.'
And so they smiled and kept talking. At first

it was painful, but soon they
got into their stride, ‘I’ll lend you my tower
so you can see what it looks like from up here,’ …
‘I’ll let you lie down in my ditch so you can
look up to the stars.’ And they’d made
quite a bit of progress when the asteroid hit.

Sermon

I see them always from my desk, the birches.
They are more real to me than any churches.

And what the truth of them may really be
it's not what's said of them in churches.

Raphael and Titian in their holy settings
are far more meaningful than churches.

I'm sure my son will marry in a church –
for form's sake – nothing to do with churches.

When my time comes, I hope they'll say some words but
not the nonsense they intone in churches.

Lunch Poem

Today I am having lunch
with Peter, Derek and Tim,
which means I am not
having lunch with Alan, Janet,
Graeme or Laura, or that man
I see by the canal, that woman
with the pushchair
and two small children,
anyone else here in Reading;
or Truss, Gove, or other
politician, any captain of industry,
postman, nursing home resident,
burglar - professional or amateur -
busy housewife, train driver,
accountant, consultant obstetrician,
Mr Jinping, his wife, our waiter,
any rhinoceros poachers or seal hunters,
air traffic controllers, anyone under
fifty-five or over seventy, or female.
What a select group we make!
Almost everyone excluded,
and I'm not even sure that Tim
will be invited next time.

The Sound Rose

Oh rose thou art sound.
The hydrogen bonds
in thy polythene heart
make a joke of decay,

and have found out our bed
of complacent ease.
Those unbreakable bonds
will our world destroy.

The Villain

after Charles of Orléans, 'Yver, vous n'etes qu'un vilain' (*c.* 1425)

Winter, you're nothing but a villain,
a hard, cold creature, of frozen days
that disappear before they start.

Spring, you are
more like a friend, your warmth
seeping into the numb mind.

And you, Summer, *are*, sometimes
insistently so, but we forgive you,
especially in the evenings.

And Autumn? Well
at least your sad beauty feeds us
while the villain lurks.

***

What? Winter! Villain no more?
Soft rain and mist?
Have you forgotten how to freeze?

Hey, Spring, turn
that heat down!
Who do you think you are?

Summer, you bastard!
Turn it off! Turn it off!
Where do you think you are?

Autumn, you dismal, dried up thing, why
the godforsaken shelves?
Come back villain!

Theories

I'm balanced on a chair,
on the tips of my toes.
I've managed to open the tap.
I'm holding a stone from the garden.

A woman is led away.
Some men have assembled
a pile of stones. Soon,
she will be dead.

I'd heard that water
wears everything away.
If I'd waited long enough
I could have proved or disproved it.

Some thought they knew
about adultery and stones.
They wanted to see if the latter
could rub away the former.

Te Deum

after Puccini, *Tosca*

I.

why, why, Lord,
why do you reward me thus?

Tosca! It is not your Lord, it is I, Scarpia,
who has built his nest in your heart.

II.

'Who are you?' she asks her son,
'Who's stolen my teeth?'

Scarpia has sidled in
and romps about in their minds

III.

Abdullah strikes David
Noam destroys Omar

Scarpia
has written both their histories

IV.

Earth shudders, buildings fall,
a huge wave …

Scarpia is heaving
tectonic plates.

Wants

I wanted love, the air sparkling
with thoughts of an as yet unseen you.

but you sent me recommendations
for paint tray liners.

I wanted somewhere nice to live
with a front door that was mine.

but you sent me a link to
a comparison site for shredders

I wanted a cure for my mum's
Alzheimer's

But you sent me a pack
of DeLonghi Universal Coffee Machine EcoDecalk Descaler.

I wanted more social care and trains that run
and doctors and teachers and pothole control

But what you said would satisfy all my desires was a 2-point
Massage Gaming Chair with XL Lumbar Cushion Headrest,
Footrest, Tall Back Full Metal Frame for Boys, Girls and
Adults, in Grey, or Black.

Coronation Poem

I was invited to a Coronation Party.
There were quiches and salad,
cake and Prosecco and a large TV.
'Does anyone want to discuss poetry?'
I shouted, 'No,' they all said, 'but
we'd love to talk about golf
and house prices.' I settled down
for an afternoon of unmitigated fun.
I hadn't enjoyed myself so much
since Brexit.

Revelation

Chris Ofili: The four horsemen of late-stage capitalism

Inequality

The exceeding tall,
because their necks are stiff
cannot perceive those
who scuttle like ants around their feet.

Deregulation

The rich ever need bathrooms
not more than two metres away
to cater for the unfortunate effects of
their appetite for the riches of the world.

Privatisation

All the good things of the world
are locked in a guarded safe.
Only the damaged
have the keys.

Austerity

Austere
are the rooms of the great, because
they have donated all their wealth
to the deserving, grateful, poor.

Autumn

Metallic slams of doors,
clacks of urgent feet:
tree surgeon, assistants,
scaffolders, nurses
hurry through the gate;
generators, arc lights,
magnifiers are
bump-hauled to the tree.

Gloves, gown, hair net,
mask – the surgeon
washes up in the mobile sink,
climbs the scaffold, and,
signalling for quiet,
examines the leaf-tree joint.

He brushes one of the steadily falling leaves
off his forearm and begins the intricate work
of incision, mending, sewing. The operation
done, the team departs, leaving a nurse to
water, feed, administer drugs, check progress
while the leaf recuperates.

Four by Four

so much depends
upon a

white
four by four

with a yellow
roof

amongst
the Christmas turkeys

Sapphic Poem

Standing at the entrance, powerful with resonance,
resonance of Empire, castles and gates,
newly anointed, bound now for Oxford, the rest
                                                            is chums

The Short and the Tall

They are so tall they are obliged to incline their heads
to go through doorways, which they accomplish
with dignity. They wear special striped or pink trousers
which are all their nannies could find to fit.
They must drink only champagne,
for it is the rising bubbles which elevate them
above the tiresome mutterings of those whose
shortness renders them invisible.

They are so short that should they come across doors,
they are unable to reach the handles and must wait
until someone lets them through. They spend their time
scratching about on floors – this keeps them short.
Appropriate materials are dropped to them
for polishing any handmade shoes
they come across down there.

The Tall vote YES, so that they may remain so.
The short vote YES so that the Tall remain tall.

Nine to Five

'[They] had human nostrils and mouths, human voices
and reason. They could marry and have children, enjoy the
pyramids or the Acropolis,'
— Georges Bataille, *Literature and Evil* (1957)

There would have been a design office,
drawing boards in rows, paper, pencils,
sharpeners, set squares, slide rules,
notebooks, manuals, books of regulations –
Buildings, *Safe Handling of Chemicals* –
and men, who'd studied hard, sat exams,
qualified, trained, who worked all day,
smoked with their friends in the breaks,
had a beer after work, went home
to wives, children and dogs, played football
on Saturdays, went to church on Sundays,
visited construction sites to check progress,
tested and commissioned the new facilities,
waited and observed as the first shipments
arrived and were processed.

Two Rivers Press has been publishing in and about Reading
since 1994. Founded by the artist Peter Hay (1951–2003),
the press continues to delight readers, local and further afield,
with its varied list of individually designed,
thought-provoking books.